avalok

Versology

From Inches to Infinity

An imprint of avalok arts

ISBN – 978-93-5525-551-8

Cover art by avalok

to
mother
nature

Mārgo gatiṃ nirdhārayati

the journey determines
the destiny

Contents

Preface

This is a seeker's diary
Not for answers
But for better questions

And my struggles to become
a compassionate witness

I am also a superstringer
I coined the word because
I couldn't find one in any dictionary
to describe my writing style
You will know why
when you join me on this journey

Consider this a forewarning
I have planted grenades across this anthology
I took the risk
I had to write them

Interrobanger

Full stops and commas
I don't use them
Colons and semicolons
I mean
What even are they?

Question marks and exclamation marks
I use them a lot
Often mash them together
into an interrobang - ‽

Life is an ‽
I am an Interrobanger

‽‽‽

Pṛthvi

Himalayan Heart

Gentle folks and tough terrains
Cold majestic mountains
reaching for the sky
Streams gurgling by
Clouds drifting low in the valley
dogs barking in narrow alley
Teapot hissing in the early morning
Warm sun-rays gladly beaming
Shepherds goading their sheep
up the green slopes so steep
Women filling water from a stream
Children with mischievous gleam
Old men with craggy faces
worn by the wind in high-up places
Bustling little meat markets
mineral water in plastic sachets
Dusty old bus snaking up the hill
passengers shrouded against the chill

Hilltop temple bells ringing
and devotees together singing
In these parts I love the most
so bury me in these mountains

???

Mountain Refuge

I walk along a steep path
climb heights that reveal
snow-capped mountains

I want to lie there
and soak in
the spirit of the nature gods
Revel in the fresh pure air

Alas!
An ordinary man
must return to tend
to his affairs

Choices are delicate
between inspiration and aspiration!

Himalayan Lesson

I was trekking in the Himalayas
Looking up
was awestruck by the heights
Was determined to reach the top
It felt inevitable

Then I stumbled and fell
Stepped on a pebble
on the path
Broke my ankle

Now I look down
while going up
Watch my feet
rather than the crown!

???

Mountainous Perceptions

I was sipping chai on a cold chilly morning
    at a ramshackle stall
    Looking at the snow-capped mountain across the vale
    Orange-hued sun rays were bouncing off the icy slopes of the peak

Soon a local villager—a shepherd
    I guessed that by his dress and gear
    sat next to me on the bench with his own hot cuppa

For quite a few long minutes
    we were watching the sun and the mountain
    weave their visual magic
    It was a dance of light and colour

After some time the shepherd turned to me and asked
    'Sir what are you looking at?'

I glanced at him
realised he was just being
welcoming and friendly

After a pause I told him

'I am trying to work out a route plan
to climb that mountain and wonder
whether I can reach the top by sunset'

He looked at me for a long moment
nodded and grinned as if he understood

Then I asked him
'Bhai Saab what were you looking at?'

'I was looking at the mountain and wondering
whether there is enough grass on the slopes
to venture up with my sheep'

He continued

‘And is there enough time to graze them
and drive them back
to the village before
the heavy downpour that’s
bound to happen this evening’

I paid for his chai and walked back
to my cosy hotel room

???

The Solo-Ride

Bend in the mountain road
What lies around the corner?
What grand vistas will appear?
Is it going to be another climb?
Or might it be a gentle descent?
Will I encounter a gentle stream
or a vicious roaring river?

It's early morning
Better start before the snow melts
Reach my next stop
before the sun hides
and the temperature drops

Will I find a place to hunker down?
A warm bed and Maggi soup?
Will a peg o' rum be offered?
Maybe a plate of hot pakoras?

Or will I have to make do with oily samosas
and a musty razai to sleep?

The charm and thrill of a solo ride
lies within the doubts and dangers

I won't give it up ever
for a 4-wheeler
an assured accommodation
and a predictable tour!

???

My Red Apache

I go for long solo rides
across India
on my Red Apache motorcycle
Reg No 2311

He has been strong
and absolutely dependable
Rarely breaks down
Low on maintenance

Has tyre punctures
occasionally
due to bad roads
Not his fault

He's been with me
for 20 years

Never refused a long ride

I will never sell him
    for a new shining model

He has been loyal to me

I need to be too

I love my Red Apache

ʔʔʔ

Sun Setting from My Terrace

These days I love watching
the sun setting from my terrace
He rises in the morning
washes all of us with his energy
Watches us going through our daily chores

He maintains a diary about us
But by evening he lets the moon
romanticise our lives
and quietly sinks below the horizon

Chuckling to himself
saying 'Enjoy your dreams
Tomorrow
I will wake you up!'

???

Kalā Kāla

Inspiration

Inspiration is like waves

Step into it

before it goes!

???

Ganesha

A paunchy non-six-pack icon
riding on a mouse with
a broken tusk weighing a ton

He laughs at obstacles
He ran around his parents
to prove a point
He is wisdom incarnate

And wisdom always winks!

Artist's Tools

An artist's easel?

A prop of compassion

The canvas?

A site for bleeding

The palette?

A confluence of passions

Brushes?

Feathers of empathy

Yet

Art is ruthless

without pity!

???

The Whaling Ship

It was simple
A seascape
Oil on canvas

Of a whaling ship
silhouetted against
a dark stormy sky
in a raging sea

I didn't get the colours right
Brushstrokes were muddy
The lighting was wrong
Perspective was shoddy

I painted the canvas black!

Went to bed
  pulled a pillow over my head
  and dreamt

Of a whaling ship
  silhouetted against
  a dark stormy sky
  in a raging sea!

???

A New World

I taught her to swim
  She'll find her shore
  and create a new world

But she knows
  I am with her
  a shadow!

???

Drowning Logic

I was writing a poem
about a frog in the well
leaping out and joining a river
To float along and reach the sea

I was interrupted by a friend telling me that
the frog will die in salt water

My poem was drowned by logic!

???

The Palette Knife

You had the
palette knife
I just
sharpened it

It's still
your knife!

???

The Moghul's Party

My close friend invited me to a party
    He was celebrating the success
    of his latest mega-project

He was my schoolmate

Then we went our own way

Now
    He is a builder
    A real estate mogul

I am a poet
    I also build

I went to his party
    My friend was glowing

Guests were drinking and dancing

Ladies were swoonable
    Music was danceable

I looked around

I didn't fit
    I am not a dancer
    I am not a Moghul

I write poetry

It was a great party

But none of them
    had bought my
    book of poems

I staggered home
    wrote another poem

???

I Write to No One

I write to no one
    Ideas shape up into sentences
    Meanings manifest themselves in verses
    I go with the Flow

I have no control
    I do not make interpretations
    All I do is spell check
    and hit the save button

Because Flow writes to no one!

???

exhilarious!

e e cummings
    (and goings)

exhilarious!

gravity
    things

f
 a
  l
   l
    only!

???

Agni

I am a Patriot

I am a patriot
    I am a congressman

I serve the country
    and my people

The other day
    I was invited to a military base
    for an event

It was a great honour

They asked me to sign on a few bombs
    I felt so proud
    I signed some more
    I was mighty pleased

I have served my country
    It was exciting
    Signing those beautiful bombs

I am a patriot
    and a congressman
    serving the country

???

Scars and Stripes

I was a young kid
    Black as night
    My papa too

I was a very curious kid
    Papa always tried his best
    to explain things to me

We lived in Philadelphia
    in the downtown area

Then came the big day
    4th of July

Dad dressed me up
    Gave me the American flag
    to wave during the parade

I was thrilled and excited

The parade was on
    when we reached

All the marchings and cheerings
    The band and its music
    was awesome

In the midst of it all

I told you I am a curious cat

I asked Dad what the flag meant
    You know about those Stars and Stripes

Dad took a deep breath
    sighed
    said
    'Son
    I don't know

about the stars
but I do know
that the whites whipped us red'

I am a kid
I didn't understand nothing
about the white and red stripes

I waved the flag
even more smartly

???

Grey

In someone's black book
blackball – black look
blackhearted – black comedy
the pot calling the kettle black
black hat hacker – black mark
black market – black mood
black day – black dog
black box – blackmail
black ops – blacklist
black Friday – blackguard
black sheep – black magic
blackleg – black handed
black deed

White lies indeed!

???

Gaza

I was writing a poem
    on the children of Gaza
    A missile hit
    and blew my poem to bits

Click

Communal riots were happening in my city
People were slaughtering each other
on an unimaginable scale
Setting poor hutments on fire
raping women
The cops were involved too

I was disturbed
Called my friend
a brilliant engineer
Expressed my concern
about the number of people being killed

He was calm and logical
He told me
'Think! We are in a big city

Consider the ratio
The deaths are just a small percentage
of the population of this city
It has to be cleaned up
Don't fret too much'

I was disappointed

A few days later
my friend called me up
His voice was shaking
He said
'Bhai do call somebody
help my family and me
The rioters have surrounded my area
We are in danger
Please call the cops'

I replied
'You're part of that small percentage

Don’t fret too much
It has to be done’

Click!

???

Gaza Gazing

'Papa Papa!
    I can't find my face!'
    She came running to me

I hugged her close
    and shut her absent eyes!

Family Man

I had a family

Things were not going well
for our community

Over the years
a kind of atmosphere was created
in the nation to fear us
Oddly this only added
to our own insecurities

But I had my family

I am no brave man
I had a wife and kids to take care of
and my old mother too

They were my family
So I changed my name
Shaved my beard off
Learnt the ways of the majority
I dressed like them
and began worshipping like them

I loved my family

All went well till
a terrible riot happened in my town
It was fuelled by hatred and distrust

I was afraid

I had a family

I was buying vegetables in the local market
A crowd with swords and lathis approached me
Screaming and shouting

They grabbed me
    dropped my pants

Now I am buried

My family had me
    no more!

???

Counting

I go to bed
thinking about Gaza
I try to sleep
Count the dead babies
instead of sheep!

???

Wedding Horse

I am a wedding horse
I am the best here in my town
Because I am a white stallion

Grooms always prefer pure white horses
I don't know why
But I am not complaining

Because my master Bhola
rakes in the moolah
during the wedding season
Therefore
he feeds me with carrots and apples

Bhola had a son Ambu
He adored me
Whenever he returned from college
He'd come to me first

caress my silky mane
and take me for a walk

I am straying

Well
Ambu got engaged
to a beautiful mare
oops
sorry

to an absolute beauty
who was as white as me
Ambu and her? Night and Day!

On the day of the wedding
I was decked up like never before
After all
Bhola owned me
The big day in Ambu's life
was about to take place

I will be the pure white stallion
to carry him to the wedding venue
I was so proud
It was an honour

I am a horse
not intelligent
not human

We were halfway to the wedding hall
the street was narrow
Then I could see in front of me
a sword wielding crowd

Of course
I couldn't see left or right
that's always been

The crowd rushed down the street towards me
I thought
'Why are they attacking me?'

One of the attackers swung his sword
    I reared in fear

When I landed
    I saw Ambu's bloody face
    lying on the ground
    looking at me

I was a white stallion

Now

I am red

???

Stench

I usually keep to myself
Avoid getting involved in neighbourhood affairs

My next-door neighbour
got married
The girl was very young and pretty
I used to watch them from my balcony
Living together happily

Months passed
Our walls were thin
So close
The sounds seeped through
I could hear the loud arguments
Not in content but in volume

I'd close my windows
    hoping to shut out the sound
    Try to go to sleep

Then one night my den
    which normally
    reeked of cigarette smoke
    was overwhelmed by a stench
    emanating from
    my neighbour's house

Dowry!

???

Cataract

He was my gardener
very old
He minded my plot
with tender care
Grew very many
types of flowers

He would come shuffling
and knock on my door
in the morning
I would prepare strong filter coffee
offer him a cup

He would water the flowers
Instruct me about what fertilisers to buy
He was very knowledgeable
about such things and more

But the thing was
his vision was impaired
Couldn't see clearly
His eyes matched his grey beard

He was too poor
to afford treatment
What little he earned
he used it to get drunk

I set up an appointment
with a doctor I knew
Told my gardener about it
I said the expenses will be borne by me

The next day he came
accompanied by a young man
Told me he was his nephew
The gardener said
the nephew will take him to the doctor

I gave him some money for the transport
and for the doctor's fees

I didn't see him for some time

Then he turned up one day
and started sobbing
Wiping his face with the tail of his turban

When asked he said the nephew
abandoned him and ran away with the money
He never reached the Doctor's clinic

I did not know what to say
Tried to console him
Gave him some more money
Then he went away
Never saw him again

Later

News reached me
    that he had drunk himself to death

Cataract!

???

Blue Hawaii Chappals

I used to go to school barefoot
I had gotten used to it
The other boys and girls
wore nice shoes and colourful chappals

My Papa had a little shop
repaired their shoes
Momma worked
in Saheb's house as a sweeper

One evening Papa called me
Patted me on the head
Gave me a pair of
Blue Hawaii chappals

Oh it was so spongy and soft
I felt I was walking on clouds
I hugged my Papa

Momma smiled
looking at me dancing

in my Blue Hawaii chappals

The next day I went to school
I didn't walk barefoot
I floated wearing my
Blue Hawaii chappals

The boys stared at me
and the girls giggled
Teacher aunty said
boy I am happy for you

I too was happy

For my Blue Hawaii chappals

Lunch time
Rupa — she was very pretty

came to me
and said I really like your
Blue Hawaii chappals

The boys were watching
As soon as Rupa went away
They rushed at me
Beat me up
tore my shirt

Threw my Blue Hawaii chappals
far into the lake
next to our school

I ran home crying
Without my

Blue Hawaii chappals

???

I MELT

I MELT
When glaciers cry

I MELT
When rivers run dry

I MELT
When there's no solidarity

I MELT
When we lose our humanity

I MELT
When my tears run dry

I MELT

???

Kāma

He was Next to Me

He was lying
next to me
Eyes closed
facing away
wishing he
was with
someone else

Then

I became
someone else

???

Karma Bites

She asked
    'Do you really love me?'

I said
    'Why?
    You have any doubts?'

I think
    I was laying the ground for
    plausible deniability

I got married to someone else

Weeks later
    I went for a walk
    I saw her coming towards me

Our eyes met
She brushed past me silently

Plausible deniability
on her part

???

Pale Blue

We were living in
Then things went south
We separated

I got married
to someone else
She did too

Years later

I bumped into her
in a mall
She was with her kid
His eyes were pale blue
Just like mine

???

It Was All Arranged

It was all arranged

I was not so thrilled
    I was going to get married
    I wanted to study more
    Graduate and become a teacher

But my Appa would not listen
    He said

'You're getting old
    Relatives are talking behind my back
    They're saying there is a lack
    that you have
    That's why you're without a suitor'

I ran to Amma tried to persuade her
    to influence Appa

to allow me to complete my college degree
Nothing worked

They found a boy
Paraded me in front of him and his family
Then they had talks with Appa
about this and that

It was all arranged

I was going to get married

I did get married as arranged

It was OK
for the first few months
My hubby worked in an IT company
Not much of a talker
Moody

Mom-in-law was the boss of the house
Her hubby was long dead and gone

Then the hints and nudges began
    My hubby told me
    about this and that they talked about
    with my Appa
    Asked me where is this and where is that

Mom-in-law joined the chorus

Then it grew louder and more accusatory
    Shouting where is this and where is that

Appa did not respond
    He said he had done all he could
    He didn't know about this and that

I wished I were not married

Then one day
    while I was cooking
    I heard something behind me

Before I could turn around
    I was burning

It was all arranged

???

I am a PhD

I did my PhD
    in social sciences
    The subject was close to my heart

I am a brilliant guy
    It was in my genes
    I researched thoroughly
    Wrote an incisive thesis
    Defended it eloquently
    in front of distinguished professors

I aced it
    Got my PhD

Now I am successful
    Teach in a prestigious college

I have a loving family
    A brilliant daughter
    She takes after me

She has moved to the USA
    She too got her PhD
    Became a professor
    Just like me

Everything was alright

Then

I got the news that
    she'd gotten married to..

I can't tell you about it

I am disappointed
    'cos I am a PhD

???

Was

I was
    a little girl

Was
    I just was

Then

My grandpa
    touched me

So did my uncle
    I thought it was love

Then they entered me

I knew something
wasn't right

Now

I wasn't

???

Embracing Demons

When reality becomes a nightmare
You're keen to embrace
even the demons in your dreams!

???

Āpas

Umachi

He was my elder brother
His friends called him
Umachi

That was not his real name
He was brilliant ebullient
Very creative
He was fair
and very handsome

Everyone in my family adored him
All eyes were on him

I was the kid brother

Not so fair not so handsome
Maybe I too was clever like him

I wished someone
    would look at me too

Nope

All eyes were on him!

I wished they would look at me
    with equal eyes

That's how it was

We grew up

He was sent abroad to do a PhD
    With father's retirement money
    He could afford to send only one

And that was Umachi

Not me

No one thought about me
My family didn't look at me

Years later

A phone call came
From Umachi's university

The caller said

'Umachi was found hanging
in his hostel room
Used a rope and ended his life'

Umachi left a note

Thanking
Amma Appa and me

Now

My family were
looking at me

???

The Crying Bench

Whenever she was disconsolate
she would sit on a bench by the bridge
Her pain and sorrow
her heartbreaks and aches
were shared with the crying bench

Her tears flowed down the edges
and cracks of the old wooden bench

Soon
Bushels of red roses grew
around the crying bench

Yet her crying did not stop
Day after day she shed copious tears
sitting on the weary old bench

Then one day
when she was feeling
extremely hopeless and abandoned
she headed towards
the crying bench by the bridge

But the crying bench was gone

She was stunned
What had happened?
How could she console herself without her crying bench?
She looked around desperately hoping
the bench had been moved to a different spot

Then she noticed
a man leaning against a tree smoking a cigarette
She approached him and asked

'Dear Sir there was a wooden bench here where I used to sit
Would you happen to know what became of it?'

The man looked at her and spoke in a soft gentle voice

'Yes my lady

I know about you and the crying bench

and about the beautiful red roses

that blossomed because of your tears

God above was watching you all the time

'The crying bench soaked up all your tears

It did as much as a wooden bench could possibly do

to absorb your sorrow and your pain

Then God realised that the crying bench had done its best

And that it wasn't enough to release your sadness'

She looked at him with questioning eyes

waiting for him to continue

'Lady

Now you have a bunch of rose bushes
Tend them with your tears
Create a beautiful garden'

???

Gudak Sitaram

Papa used to take me to the market
to buy house things in KGF

He would make me sit on the cycle crossbar
it was a tall 24-inch Raleigh
Military green in colour
Made in England
With a star-shaped brass license plate

The road to the market was steep
His pedalling efforts
breathed on my neck
It felt good

I would ask him
Papa where are we going?
He always replied
Gudak Sitaram

I never understood what he was talking about

I mean
What is
Gudak Sitaram?
A person or a place?

We would buy groceries
and he would buy a candy for me

Going back was easier
Papa showed his skills
by lifting his hands off the handlebars

I used to get scared
But I liked it
I used to ask him
Is this Gudak Sitaram?
He would just laugh it off

Now Papa is being cared for
He can neither ride nor walk
he can't even lift his arms
A nurse is around him
To bathe him and take him to the toilet

I haven't heard him mention
Gudak Sitaram for a long time now

Now
he's gone

Maybe he was
Gudak Sitaram!

???

Manipedia

We just knew him as Mani

He had a corner petty shop
    selling magazines and toffees

Mani angadi
    It was our HQ

All of us used to meet there
    in the evening
    Gossiped and shared beedis
    talked cricket
    ogled at aunties

Some were studying
    Some were moping
    Some were coping
    We were all hoping

Friends left messages with him
    He knew who was in town
    Who got married
    and who got into trouble

He was Manipedia

Before Wikipedia was born

I am old now
    Retired and tired

Where are they now?
    Who is alive
    Who is dead?

Mani angadi
    had no answers

Because Mani
    is no more

???

He was Gandhi

He was Gandhi
Had large ears
Near to being ugly
Was physically weak
Wore a piece of khadi
He had a broken smile
Walked around in chappals

What mattered was
what he had inside
An unbreakable will
Was steadfast and forthright

Above all
Adherence
to truth and non-violence

He was Gandhi

Mīṇḍ

Paintings
poetry
and stories for company

Caressing my drink
I sink into the ambience

Listening to soft somnolent blues
The guitarist's fingers gliding across the strings

The fears of yesterday
and anxieties of tomorrow
melt away

Cos I am happily
swimming in the Now!

???

Passing Show

He was single
Not related
But he was adopted
as part of the family

His name was Rajam

He had fought
in the Burma war
He became a journalist
when he came back
to Madras

He was witty
had friends who were wittier

I was just a young kid
admiring Rajam and his friends

Rajam used to give me money
send me to the petty shop
to buy his favourite
Passing Show cigarettes

Rajam would then tip me
so that I could buy sweets

I grew up
graduated
Pursued my career
I was so busy
I forgot Rajam

Now I am successful
Settled

Got the news
that Rajam died
A car hit him
while he was alighting
from a bus

Nobody in my family
mentions him now

Rajam came
and went

They forgot him

But Rajam
is still with me

???

What woke me up?

A ray of light from the morning sun
    woke me up from a dream
    or was it the grinning mask
    within the dream?

How will I know
    until I continue to dream?

I went back to sleep

???

Where Do I Go?

In my dream
　I was floating like a feather
　Buffeted by the wind
　hither and thither

I woke up and wondered
　'Where do I go from here?'

Before walking out
　I checked the weather!

???

The Paper Boat

I am a paper boat

I have no control

I trust the river to connect me

with my soul!

???

Puzzled Life

What a puzzle is this life

Before you find its meaning
    you're bent and sent
    elsewhere!

???

Trapped

A frog in the well
An animal in a zoo
A bird in a cage
You're in the same situation too!

???

Akāśa

Masks & Mindfulness

I have this odd little hobby
of collecting macabre masks
I nest them among the mundane
Scissors pens and paper frogs

Placed just so
Waiting Watching

And when I drift
mindless in my motions
they jolt me awake

A sudden stare
A crooked smile
and a whisper

'Be here now'

The Unfinished Art

Yama came to fetch me
I looked him in the eye
He said 'Your time's up'

I said 'Can't you see?
My painting is not yet complete'

He glanced at my canvas
And let me be!

While leaving he said
'I'll come back when you've finished painting'

I laughed at him and said
'A painter is never finished with his art'

???

The Unguru

I heard about a wise man
Who lived on top of a mountain
People said he spoke little
but taught a lot

They called him the Unguru
Because he was the exact opposite
Of those pontificating preachers

I was eager to find out

I found him and paid my respects
I said I wanted answers
for a few questions
that were troubling me

The Unguru didn't speak
He gave me a piercing look

Nodded and then waved his hand
to indicate that I can proceed

My first question was
'What is Happiness?'
He closed his eyes for a moment
Then pointed to the setting Sun

My second question was
'What is sadness then?'
He pointed in another direction
And I could see the moon appearing

'What is this thing called Life?'
I asked him and he smiled
Pointed at the floating clouds
Which were constantly changing shape

Then I asked him
'What is the Purpose of Life?'
He pointed to the gushing river
below flowing ever so gracefully

I asked him some more
  'What happens when we Die?'
  He pointed towards the horizon
  where the river merged into the ocean

I asked him one last question
  'Who am I and where do I come from?'
  And he pointed to a shining star

I took his blessings and left

???

Where Do Masks Go?

I keep wondering
    If all the masks are replaced
    with my paintings

Where do they go?

Do they vanish into the shadows
    or slip into the strokes I make?

Will I ever meet them again?

???

Celebration

The wisest ones are those who
bring you in and send you away
Not the priests or pundits
who recite by rote obscure deceptive soundbites

Celebrations of your journey are truly conducted
by Midwives and Funeraries

???

ICU

Mom was supine in the ICU
    Her hands were cold
    and veins blue

Bills were mounting up
    Doctors told me to pray
    Said hope for a miracle

How long will she be in a coma
    I wanted an assurance
    None came forth

Finally
    I asked them to pull the plug

Who killed my mother?
    Is it me? Or...

???

One So Dear to Me

He was our son
the apple of our eyes
So affectionate obedient and dutiful
In our old age thought he'd take care of us
Dear Lord
How can You do this?
Why did You take him away from us?

He was my friend
philosopher and guide
Someone with whom I could enjoy and share
When needed thought he'd always be there
Tell me Lord
Why did You do this?
Took him away
One so special to me?

He was my partner
and my companion for life
So loving caring kind and patient
Thought he would be with me forever
Dear Lord
How could You be so cruel?
Took him away
One who was bound to me?

He was my dear father
and my beacon
So doting playful
used to make me laugh
Thought he'd be around to see me bloom
Tell me Lord
Why did You do this?
Snatched him away
One so needed by me?

I hear you all please try to understand
Each one of you is a part of Me

I send each one of you down to earth
with an opportunity and a challenge

To become a perfect soul to please Me

As a grain in a shell becomes a pearl
As coal under pressure turns into a diamond

Each soul is expected during life's journey
to be polished into a clear shining mirror
reflecting the glory of Me

He was eager and conscious of his purpose
I saw Myself in him sooner than expected

Hear Me mother daughter partner friend
Please forgive Me
I had to take him back
Because he became equally dear to Me

???

Author's note

This poem was written to honour the memory of my close friend—a scientist

He tragically died in an accident

He was very young

???

Leafing

I am leafing
Through my scribbled notes
I am leafing through
my unwritten books

I am leafing through
my dreams and nightmares
I am tired of leafing
Just leaving

???

Camping Under Stars

I was in a camping site
It was night and I lay down
and looked up at the stars

They were closer to me than my friends!

???

Done

Life—

lived it

leafed through it

left it

???

My Fav Mask

My fav face was there
    when I reached

Heaven is a calm sea
    where masks are beached!

???

Stars and dust last

You don't

???

Note from avalok

Interrobanged!

I sent my fully refined
Versology manuscript
to a publishing house

I hired them to give
the final touch to Versology
To polish and prepare it
Get it ready for printing

It is a modern book of verses

The central philosophy
of the book is explained
in "Interrobanger"

Versology contains
no commas and full stops

It is a stylistic choice

The team at the publishing house
while editing the poem
added full stops and commas
all over including the Interrobanger poem?!

This happened with this book

Versology barely managed to escape
from the clutches of the editorial team
with its vision intact!

Exhilarious?!

⸮⸮⸮

About the Author

avalok

Artist Poet

Compassionate witness

Compulsive coddiwompler

Navigating life with purpose

Floating towards the unknown

Art is about stretching canvas inches to infinity

Fleeting moments into light years

Connect with me

Imprint

avalok arts

Bengaluru

India